OCS Study
MMS 2002-026

Socioeconomic Baseline and Projections of the Impact of an OCS Onshore Base for Selected Florida Panhandle Communities

Volume III: User's Guide for the Model

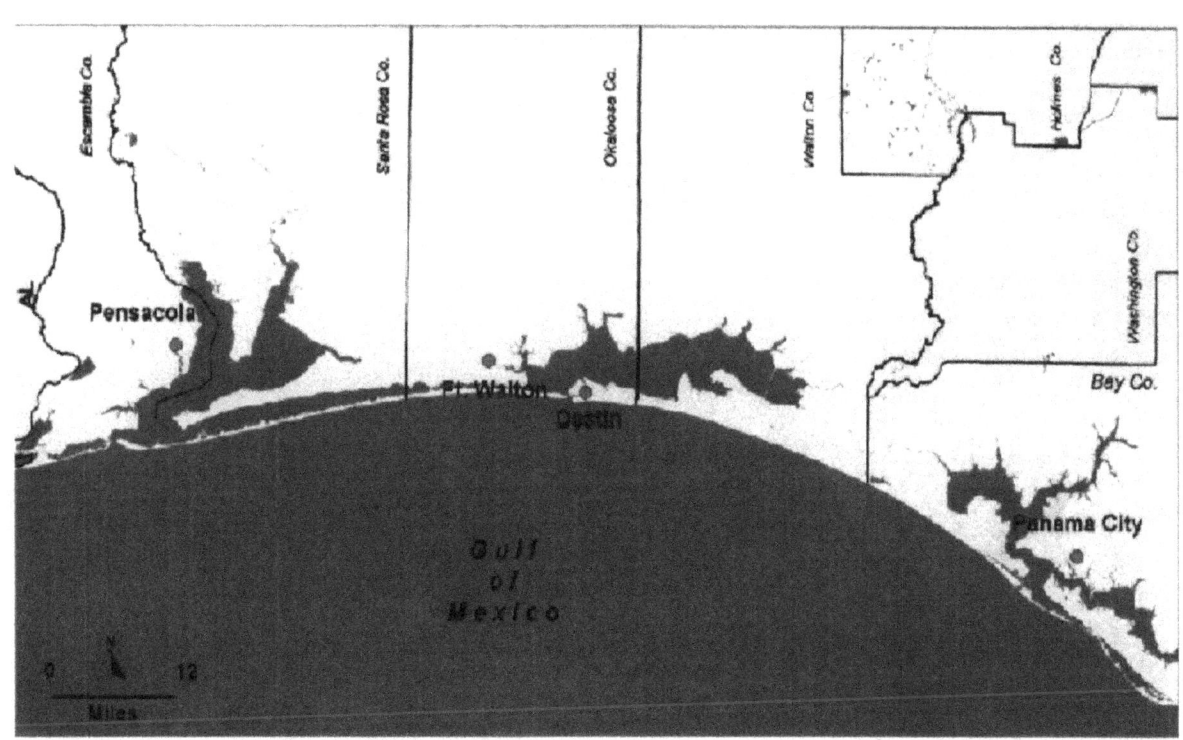

U.S. Department of the Interior
Minerals Management Service
Gulf of Mexico OCS Region

OCS Study
MMS 2002-026

Socioeconomic Baseline and Projections of the Impact of an OCS Onshore Base for Selected Florida Panhandle Communities

Volume III: User's Guide for the Model

Authors

Ronald T. Luke
Eric S. Schubert
Greg Olsson
Research and Planning Consultants, Inc.
Austin, Texas

and

F. Larry Leistritz
North Dakota State University

Prepared under MMS Contract
1435-01-96-CT-30821
by
Research and Planning Consultants, Inc.
Austin, Texas

Published by

U.S. Department of the Interior
Minerals Management Service
Gulf of Mexico OCS Region

New Orleans
May 2002

DISCLAIMER

This model and user's guide were prepared under contract between the Minerals Management Service (MMS) and Research and Planning Consultants, Inc. This report has been technically reviewed by the MMS, and it has been approved for publication. Approval does not signify that the contents necessarily reflect the views and policies of the MMS, nor does mention of trade names or commercial products constitute endorsement or recommendation for use. It is, however, exempt from review and compliance with the MMS editorial standards.

REPORT AVAILABILITY

Extra copies of this model and user guide may be obtained from the Public Information Unit (Mail Stop 5034) at the following address:

U.S. Department of the Interior
Minerals Management Service
Gulf of Mexico OCS Region
Public Information Unit (MS 5034)
1201 Elmwood Park Boulevard
New Orleans, Louisiana 70123-2394

Telephone: (504) 736-2519 or
1-800-200-GULF

CITATION

Suggested citation:

Luke, R. T., E.S. Schubert, G. Olsson, and F.L. Leistritz. 2002. Socioeconomic Baseline and Projection Model for Selected Florida Panhandle Communities, Volume III: User's Guide for the Model. U.S. Dept. of the Interior, Minerals Management Service, Gulf of Mexico OCS Region, New Orleans, LA. OCS Study MMS 2002-026. 32 pp.

TABLE OF CONTENTS

LIST OF FIGURES

LIST OF TABLES

MMS Socioeconomic Projection Model for
Selected Panhandle Communities

Background Issues

Purpose of Model

The National Environmental Policy Act of 1969 (NEPA) and the Outer Continental Shelf Lands Act, as amended in 1978 (OCSLA), mandate the Federal Government to consider the effects of major Federal actions on the human environment. The Minerals Management Service (MMS) Environmental Studies Program (ESP) supports the Department of Interior's management decision process for the Outer Continental Shelf (OCS) by providing scientific information.

The MMS, in its most recent Five-Year Plan (1997-2002), stated its intention to lease tracts of water in the western edge of the Eastern Planning Area of the Gulf of Mexico. In January 1999, the MMS announced that this sale, now known as Lease Sale 181, will take place in 2002. (For more detail on Lease Sale 181, go to the MMS website http://www.mms.gov/gom.) Lease Sale 181 and the proposed Destin Dome offshore natural gas project located 25 miles south of Pensacola have renewed the debate on the costs and benefits of offshore oil and gas drilling in the Eastern Gulf of Mexico among stakeholders in the Florida Panhandle. While RPC and the MMS both believe that Alabama is the most likely location for any onshore support activities in the western part of the Eastern Planning Area, a possibility exists that limited onshore support activities might occur in Panama City or Pensacola that could have a socioeconomic impact on the five counties of the Florida Panhandle: Bay, Escambia, Okaloosa, Santa Rosa, and Walton.

Because the experience of Texas and Louisiana has indicated substantial social and economic impacts from Outer Continental Shelf (OCS) activity are possible, the MMS wanted to investigate the potential impacts on affected communities in the Eastern Gulf of Mexico. In trying to address the concerns and questions of stakeholders in the Florida Panhandle, RPC has conducted research and prepared a model that provides users with plausible quantitative projections of these concerns. In particular, the MMS Florida Panhandle Model can compare the economic value of potential OCS activity generated in the Florida Panhandle by an onshore support base with the economic value of the area's key industries: the military and tourism.

Description of Model

Research and Planning Consultants (RPC) wrote the MMS Socioeconomic Projection Model for Selected Communities in the Florida Panhandle (MMS Florida Panhandle Model) as a set of three economic-demographic submodels. Each submodel represents one of the metropolitan, or impact, areas within the Florida Panhandle. RPC has defined the three metropolitan areas, Fort Walton Beach, Panama City, and Pensacola, as follows:

1

Fort Walton Beach:	Okaloosa and Walton Counties
Panama City:	Bay County
Pensacola:	Escambia and Santa Rosa Counties

For purposes of the MMS Florida Panhandle Model, RPC assumes that the economic impacts of OCS activity would only occur in the metro area where the support activity occurs.

This economic-demographic model projects both baseline and impact-related economic activity through the interaction of local output and labor force. Migration into and out of the Florida Panhandle is the force that restores equilibrium in the local economy. Economic activity drives changes in the population under age 65 (i.e., working-age people and their families) through migration. Baseline projections every five years from 1995 through 2045 indicate the levels of economic activity and population for the three metro areas that would likely occur with a continuation of present socioeconomic trends.

As part of RPC's stakeholder analysis, a number of stakeholders expressed concerns to RPC that locating an onshore base in the Florida Panhandle could negatively impact the region's military and tourism industries. Research findings indicate that the level of proposed OCS activity serviced by an onshore base in the Florida Panhandle probably would not impact the military or tourism in the region. RPC has built the option of quantifying these negative impacts into the model, however, for the benefit of these stakeholders without agreeing with their premise that such negative impacts would occur.

RPC examined the impacts of OCS activity on the fishing industry, but commercial fishing is a very small employer in the Florida Panhandle, and recreational fishing is closely linked to the tourism industry. Therefore, this model does not address explicitly the potential impacts on the fishing industry.

For more detailed information on the structure, assumptions, and sources of information RPC used to build this model and produce the baselines, please read the Final Report associated with this project.

Socioeconomic Baseline of the Florida Panhandle

RPC calibrated its model so that the baselines for the three areas were consistent with published sources used by local and state government officials in making their planning decisions. As part of its project design, RPC prepared baselines for each of the three areas that approximated the population projections developed by two independent sources: the U.S. Bureau of Economic Analysis (BEA) and the University of Florida's Bureau of Economic and Business Research (BEBR). BEBR used a cohort-component model to project population without the direct interaction with an economic module that would take into account changing economic conditions.

In 1995, the Bureau of Economic Analysis developed their most recent set of projections of employment and earnings commonly known as the "OBERS," which the Army Corps of Engineers and other Federal agencies use for long-term water development projects. In these projections, which run from 1995 through 2045, the BEA started with U.S. Census population projections on a national level and used long-term shares in employment by industry group to allocate employment and population among states and metropolitan statistical areas across the United States.

The MMS Florida Panhandle Model provides users with a tabular description of the baseline output, employment, population, and migration for each of the three metropolitan areas. (See below).

Potential OCS Activity in the Eastern Gulf of Mexico

Lease Sale 181
According to MMS projections, the levels of OCS production from Lease Sale 181 in the Eastern Planning Area are small compared to the projected production levels from leases in the Western and Central Gulf of Mexico scheduled for auction in 1997-2002. The MMS projects that offshore activity associated with Lease Sale 181 will have a life of forty years, including exploration. Projected output is 500 to 810 billion cubic feet of natural gas and 30 to 60 million barrels of oil pumped from five to eight platforms and twenty to thirty wells. Based on information that MMS provided to RPC, this report assumes that hydrocarbon production starts in 2010 and ends by 2040. The MMS anticipates that the production arising from Lease Sale 181 will not require a new pipeline landfall and that an existing shore base in Mobile, Alabama, will service offshore rigs in the lease area.

Destin Dome
The Destin Dome project consists of eleven leased blocks of water 25 miles off the coast of Pensacola jointly owned by Chevron, Murphy Exploration and Production, and Conoco, Inc. Exploratory wells have confirmed large quantities of natural gas but no oil. According to the Development and Production Plan that Chevron submitted to the MMS in 1997, the project will have between 12 to 21 active wells and is slated to begin production in the year 2000. The onshore support base for drilling and production will be located at an existing base on the Theodore Ship Channel near Mobile, Alabama, or Bayou Cassotte in Pascagoula, Mississippi. Chevron does not anticipate that expansion of any onshore support base will be necessary to support the Destin Dome project. A central processing facility will be installed offshore near the production wells and move by pipelines in Federal waters to existing gas plants in Mobile, Alabama.

The Potential Scope of OCS-Related Activity in the Florida Panhandle
This model measures the hypothetical socioeconomic impact of locating an onshore service base in the Florida Panhandle instead of Mobile, Alabama. RPC's research indicates that few economic incentives are present to drive OCS support industries into the Florida Panhandle at the

projected levels of OCS development in the Eastern Gulf of Mexico. Support bases are most efficient when close to offshore wells and handling multiple projects at the same time, rather than the one or two projects that this model analyzes.

But even if the offshore industry were to establish an onshore base in the Florida Panhandle, established bases in Texas, Louisiana, and Alabama would likely service most of the specialized needs of offshore exploration and production. Expansion of offshore facilities and services into the Florida Panhandle likely would come in the form of an onshore support base that would service offshore platforms during the operation and maintenance portion of any offshore oil and gas development. The potential impacts in the Florida Panhandle would likely be in a different form than often associated with oil and gas development. Direct socioeconomic impacts likely will be smaller than those that have occurred in the Western and Central Gulf of Mexico.

If the oil industry were to locate an onshore service base in the Florida Panhandle, the operators of the base would need to import many O&M supplies from outside the region, limiting the potential economic benefits to the Florida Panhandle. As a result of the limited scope of operations and the limited production in the Eastern Gulf of Mexico, operations and maintenance (O&M) activity from the developed wells will generate at most about twenty million dollars in direct expenditures in any given year, and in some scenarios not reach twelve million in any year (Table 1).

Table 1

**Potential Operation and Maintenance Expenditures in the Florida Panhandle
(direct expenditures only in millions of dollars)**

Sector	2000	2005	2010	2015	2020	2025	2030	2035	2040	2045
Lease Sale 181 Scenarios										
Minimum Threshold	0.00	0.00	1.26	4.27	6.48	5.69	5.06	3.64	0.00	0.00
Reasonable Maximum	0.00	0.00	2.17	7.28	11.16	9.76	8.68	6.19	0.00	0.00
No OCS Activity Results from Sale	0.00	0.00	0.00	0.00	0.00	0.00	0.00	0.00	0.00	0.00
Destin Dome Scenario	7.90	20.70	14.20	7.90	4.50	0.00	0.00	0.00	0.00	0.00
Maximum Impact in Model										
Reasonable Maximum	0.00	0.00	2.17	7.28	11.16	9.76	8.68	6.19	0.00	0.00
Destin Dome	7.90	20.70	14.20	7.90	4.50	0.00	0.00	0.00	0.00	0.00
Total	**7.90**	**20.70**	**16.37**	**15.18**	**15.66**	**9.76**	**8.68**	**6.19**	**0.00**	**0.00**

Ports of Pensacola and Panama City

Background
The study area has two major, deep water ports that would make the best locations for an onshore support base in the Florida Panhandle: the Port of Pensacola and the Port of Panama City. Because Fort Walton Beach does not have such a deep-water facility, that impact area would not benefit directly from locating an onshore base in the Florida Panhandle. While the Port of Pensacola has a history extending back into the nineteenth century, the present-day location of the Port of Panama City opened only after World War II. The ports of Pensacola (ranked 78th) and Panama City (ranked 62nd) in 1995 were among the top 100 U.S. ports in the dollar value of goods exported. They ranked 120th and 100th, respectively, in the value of imports.

User-Conflicts and Benefits
The two ports would benefit from hosting an onshore support base. Both ports appear to have enough spare capacity to handle the business from Lease Sale 181 or Destin Dome. The Port of Panama City served as an onshore support base for exploratory drilling in the Gulf of Mexico in the early 1980s and in 1990 and has an adjacent industrial park that houses industries associated with offshore oil and gas industry.

Tourism

Background
The development of the Florida Panhandle as a major tourist area began in the mid-1930s and grew rapidly after World War II, becoming what is now a key industry in the Florida Panhandle. Traditionally a place in the "Old South" to go for swimming and fishing, the Florida Panhandle is often called the "Southern Riviera."

"Sugar-white" beaches, fishing, other water-based activities, and natural habitats are key parts of the tourist experience in the Florida Panhandle, a type of tourism known as ecotourism. In the mid-1990s, the area attracted 10 million visitors annually who generated $1.5 billion of business. Heavily visited by automobile traffic, the Florida Panhandle represents one of the few high quality beach areas available to many visitors in the southeastern U. S., with high proportions coming from Alabama, Arkansas, Louisiana, Mississippi, and Texas.

User-Conflicts and Benefits
Though a small onshore base in the Florida Panhandle would cause few direct user-conflicts with the tourism industry, stakeholder views of the impacts of OCS development on tourism will result as much from perceived reality as from the evolution of actual events. Because tourism in the area is largely based on the aesthetics of the environment, environmental issues likely will dominate any debate on the benefits and costs of OCS development. The major threats likely to be perceived from OCS-related activity are environmental. Many stakeholders in tourism and related industries in the Florida Panhandle fear that such development could depreciate the aesthetic quality or use of beaches, of coastal waters, and of fish and other wildlife.

Military

Background
The military has had a substantial presence in the Florida Panhandle since World War II. The four main military installations in the study area are the Pensacola Naval Air Station, Eglin Air Force Base (Fort Walton Beach), Tyndall Air Force Base, and the Coastal Systems Station (both in Panama City). The three air bases use the Northern Gulf of Mexico as a weapons testing and training range. The Coastal Systems Station uses St. Andrew's Bay and the nearby waters of the Gulf of Mexico for testing and training in antisubmarine and underwater warfare. The military employs over 30,000 people in the Florida Panhandle economy, accounting for 8.6 percent all nonfarm employment in 1995, compared with only 1.5 percent in the United States as a whole. These bases were largely untouched by the downsizing of the military in the 1990s and are expected to remain an important part of the Florida Panhandle economy for the foreseeable future.

User-Conflicts and Benefits
The air bases would have potential conflicts with supply boats and helicopters crossing their testing ranges, but stipulations in any oil leases in the Eastern Gulf of Mexico put the onus of these conflicts on the oil industry. The Coastal Systems Station expressed a concern that a high level of supply boat traffic from the Port of Panama City might interfere with its operations, but the level associated with servicing the proposed projects appears to fall below that threshold. Again, the oil industry likely would need to accommodate local military operations.

Socioeconomic Impacts of OCS Activity

The socioeconomic impacts of development projects and programs can be categorized in a number of ways. One classification of such impacts identifies (1) *economic* impacts (changes in an area's employment and output), (2) *demographic* impacts (changes in the size and composition of the area's population), (3) *public service* impacts (changes in the demand for, and availability of, public services and facilities), and (4) *fiscal* impacts (changes in revenues and costs among local governmental jurisdictions). The model presents these types of impacts in a series of reports. (See below).

Operating the Model

Hardware Requirements

The MMS Florida Panhandle Model runs on Microsoft Excel 97 in a Windows 95, 98, or NT environment. A minimum of 32 megabytes of memory is required. The operation of the program also requires the use of a mouse.

Model Installation

To install the model, users insert the Diskette 1 into their computers, choose the "RUN" command in Windows, type "a:\setup.exe" for the diskette and follow the directions on screen. The installation program will provide users with a series of dialogue boxes to assist the user with the installation of the model.

Program Files

When installed, the model contains a program file (CONTROL.XLS) , nine "read-only" files Microsoft Excel files, and various text files. These files are located in the specific subdirectories that the installation program creates on the hard drives of the users. If any of these files are missing from their designated subdirectories, the model may not operate properly.

Operating the Model

The model can run only in Microsoft Excel 97 or later. Once opened, users need no further knowledge of Microsoft Excel to operate the model, as RPC has designed the MMS Florida Panhandle model to run on a series of menus that prompt users to choose a scenario, learn background material associated with the analysis, and generate reports. Please note that the model is "read only."

To open the model, users should point their mouses to click the "Start" button at the lower left-hand corner of the screen, then go to "Programs", "MMS Florida Panhandle Model"." The model will open Microsoft Excel automatically. The model may ask if users want to "enable" or "disable" macros before continuing. Users must choose the "enable" button or the model may not work. The model will then take users to the first screen in the model.

When operating the model, users should consider closing other open Microsoft Excel files and applications such as word processors. The MMS Florida Panhandle model requires 32 megabytes of memory in order to generate scenarios. Open files and applications will reduce the amount of memory available for the model and could reduce the operating speed of the model.

User Options and Procedures

The model will have three menus through which the user will navigate: the Introductory Page, the Main Menu, and the Scenario Builder.

Introductory Page: This page will be the first menu that users will see whenever they open the model. (See next page for a picture of this menu.) This menu contains three option buttons:

    1.   Main Menu: This choice will take users to the Main Menu. (See Figure 1)

    2.   Purpose of the Model: This choice will open a text page that will provide users with background information on the model.

3.   Exit Model: This choice will close the MMS Florida Panhandle Model and return the model to its defaults. The model will return users to an open Microsoft Excel program.

Figure 1. MMS Florida Panhandle Model - Screen 1.

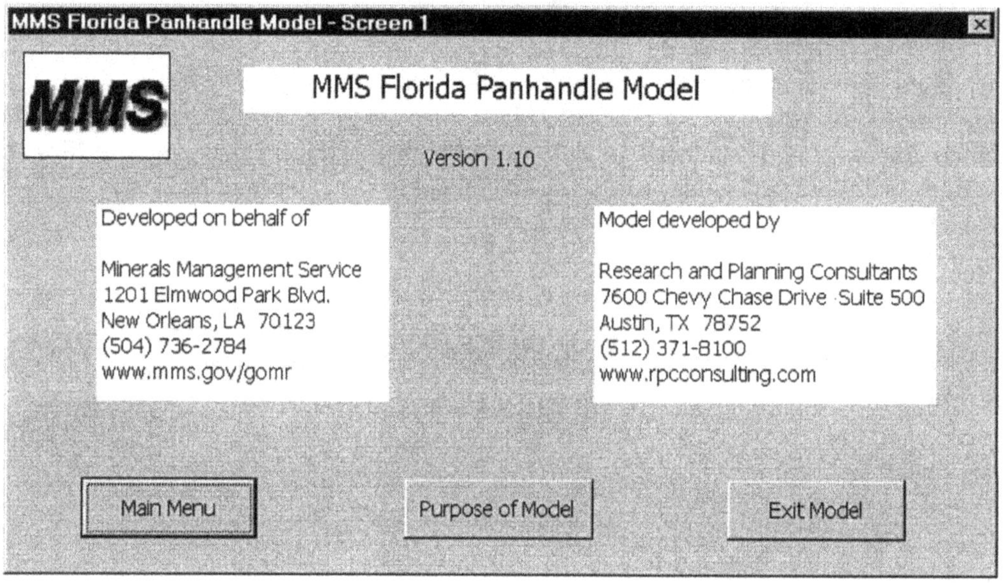

Main Menu: The Main Menu contains a Message Box and five options buttons described below. (See Figure 2).

1.   Build a Scenario: This choice takes users to the four-part Scenario Builder. (See below).

2.   Run MMS Model: After users have built a scenario, this choice prompts the model to calculate the results. The Message Box will inform users when they may see the results of the scenario they have chosen.

3.   Print Reports: After users have run a scenario, users can print a series of reports that illustrate the socioeconomic impacts of their scenario on the impact area.

4.   Baseline of the Model: This button will open a text box that discusses the baseline economic and demographic projections for the Florida Panhandle that the model uses.

5.   Exit Menu: This choice will close the MMS Florida Panhandle Model and return the model to its defaults. The model will return user to the Introductory Page.

8

Figure 2. MMS Florida Panhandle Model - Main Menu Screen.

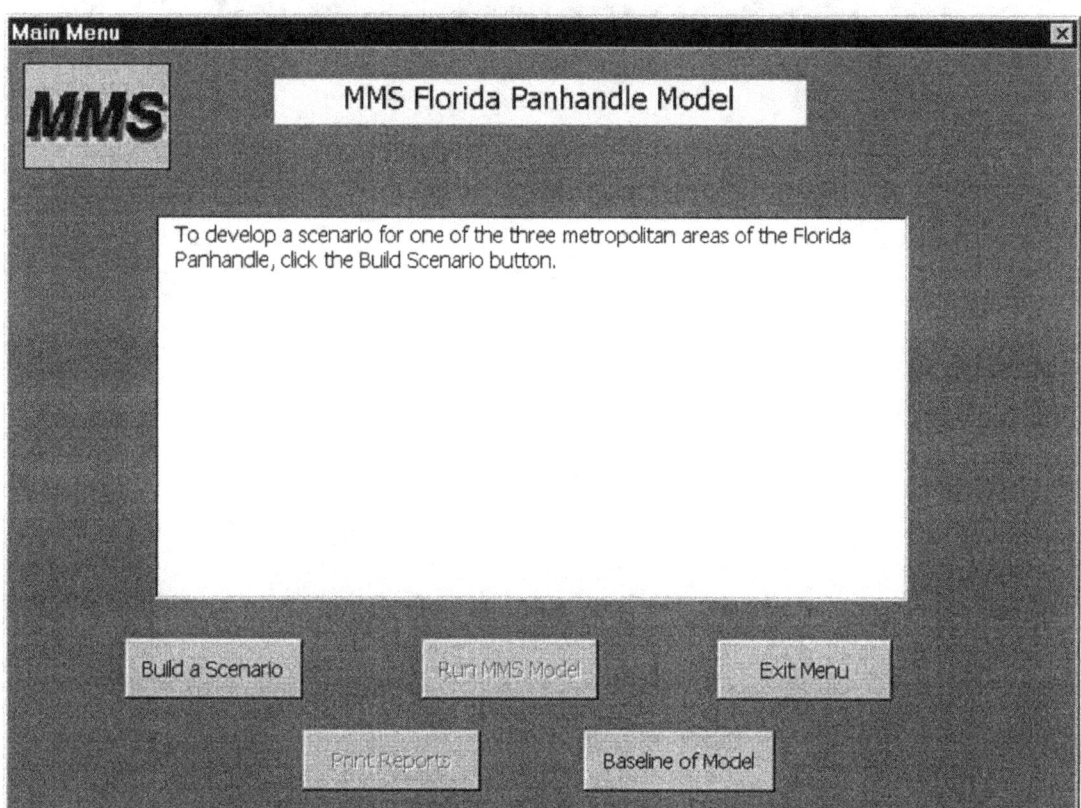

Scenario Builder: The Scenario Builder is a four-part menu that allows users to generate a variety of scenarios and provides an explanation of the various choices the model provides.   The four pages within the Scenario Builder menu are as follows: Impact Area, OCS Activity, Tourism, and Military. Users should point and click the mouse on one of the titles to review the options on each page.

The following is a description of the options available to users on each of the four pages of the Scenario Builder.

Impact Area

Users choose among one of three geographic areas - Fort Walton Beach, Panama City, or Pensacola (Figure 3). The user must choose one of the three before the model grants the user access to the OCS Activity, Tourism, and Military pages.

The "Background" option button prompts a text page that provides users with a brief background on local deep water ports and their potential for hosting an onshore service base.

Figure 3. Impact Scenario - Impact Area.

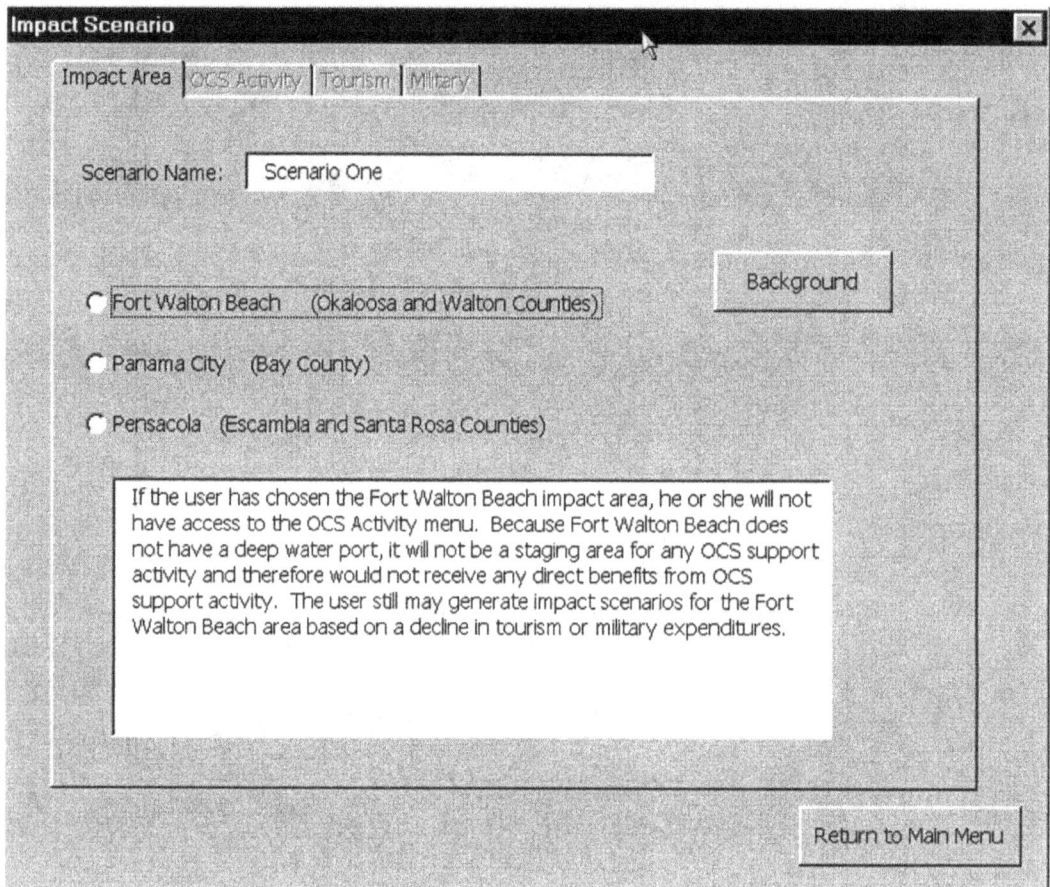

OCS Activity

The model generates scenarios that estimate the impact of OCS support activity on the Florida Panhandle from Destin Dome, Lease Sale 181, both, or neither (Figure 4).

i.   Panama City and Pensacola:

Destin Dome: If a user wants to have an onshore support base in the Florida Panhandle service the offshore platforms involved in the Destin Dome project, he should put a check in the "Destin Dome" by pointing his mouse at the box and clicking.

Lease Sale 181: Users can choose from one of the three programmed scenarios or develop their own. To choose one of the three programmed scenarios, users need to click the "Programmed Scenarios" button with their mouses and then choose one of the three scenarios listed in the box to the side of the button. The choices are as follows:

(1)   Minimum Threshold
(2)   Reasonable Maximum
(3)   No OCS Activity Serviced in the Florida Panhandle

If users want to develop their own OCS scenarios, they should click the "User-Defined Scenario" button with the mouse and then choose a number from 1 to 100. The output chosen falls between the "Minimum Threshold" and "Reasonable Maximum" scenarios, with "0" being equal to the "Minimum Threshold" scenario and 100 being equal to the "Reasonable Maximum" scenario. The number "50", for instance, would represent output from Lease Sale 181 that would be the midpoint between the "Minimum Threshold" and "Reasonable Maximum" scenarios.

ii.   Fort Walton Beach: If users choose the Fort Walton Beach impact area, they will see a blank screen on the OCS Activity menu. The screen is blank because Fort Walton Beach does not have a deep water port, it will not be a staging area for any OCS support activity and therefore would not receive any direct benefits from OCS support activity.

Users may generate impact scenarios for the Fort Walton Beach area based on a decline in tourism or military expenditures. (See below)

The "Scenario Description" option button prompts a text page referring to Table 1 in the User's Guide.

Figure 4. Impact Scenario - OCS Activity.

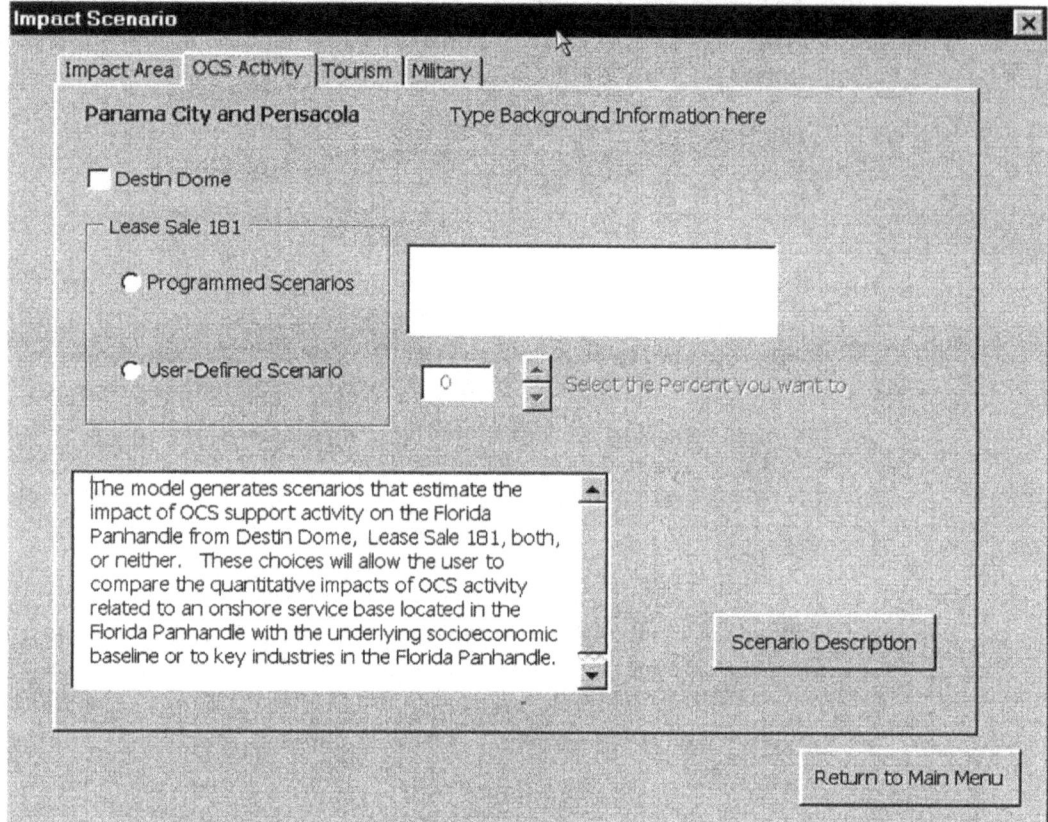

Tourism

As part of RPC's stakeholder analysis, a number of stakeholders expressed concerns to RPC that locating an onshore base in the Florida Panhandle could negatively impact the region's tourist business. Research findings indicate that the level of proposed OCS activity serviced by an onshore base in the Florida Panhandle probably would not impact tourism in the region. RPC has built the option of quantifying these negative impacts, however, for the benefit of these stakeholders without agreeing with their premise that such negative impacts would occur.

Users have a choice of two types of impacts on tourism in the Florida Panhandle:
- a. Change in the projected level of tourism
- b. Change in the growth rate of tourism

Users can select negative impacts that range from zero to twenty percent of the projected level of tourism or the projected growth rate of tourism (Figure 5). Users may start the impact as early as 2000 or as late as 2040. The defaults in the model are zero percent for both the projected level and growth rate of tourism, the levels consistent with the findings of RPC's research.

The "Background" option button prompts a text page that provides users with a summary of the tourism industry and likely user-conflicts between OCS support activity and tourism in the Florida Panhandle.

Figure 5. Impact Scenario - Tourism.

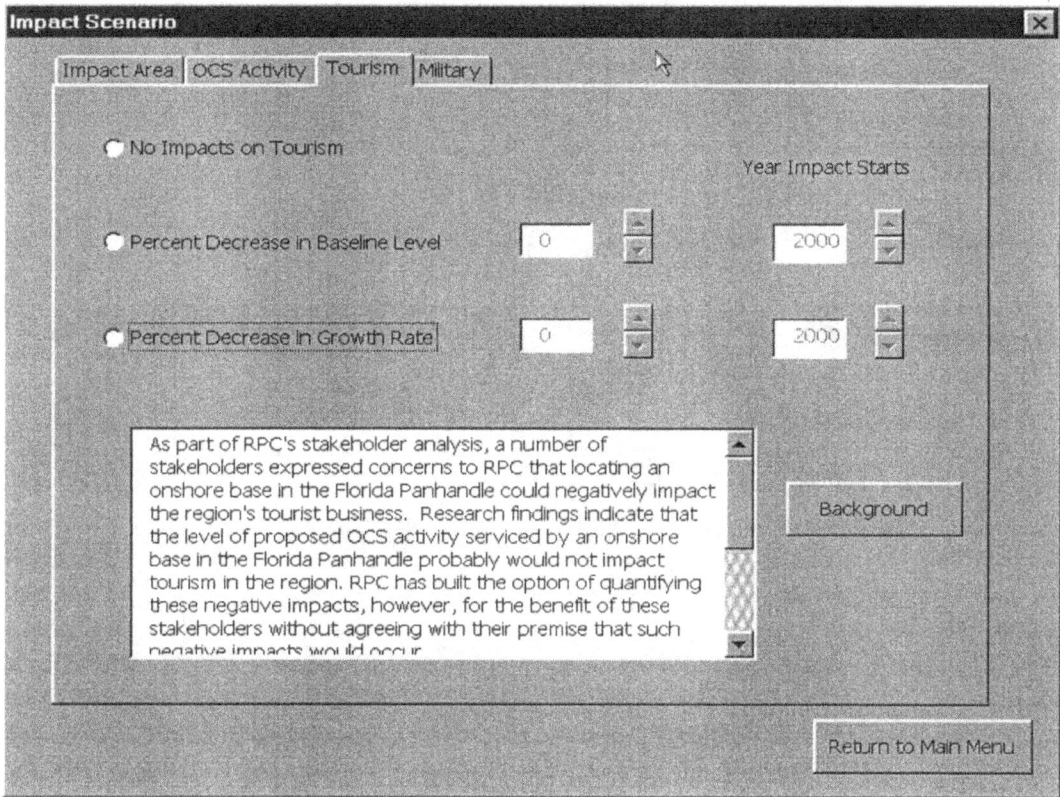

Military

As part of RPC's stakeholder analysis, a number of stakeholders expressed concerns to RPC that locating an onshore base in the Florida Panhandle could negatively impact the region's military expenditures. Research findings indicate that the level of proposed OCS activity serviced by an onshore base in the Florida Panhandle would not impact military expenditures in the region. RPC has built the option of quantifying such a negative impact, however, for the benefit of these stakeholders without agreeing with their premise that such negative impacts would occur.

Users can select negative impacts that range from zero to twenty percent of the projected level of military expenditures (Figure 6). Users may start the impact as early as 2000 or as late as 2040. The default impact on the military in the model is zero, the level consistent with the findings of RPC's research.

The model's "baseline" report presents RPC's projections of baseline military expenditures and employment for each region. The "Background" option button provides a brief summary of what is in the User's Guide on this issue.

Figure 6. Impact Scenario - Military.

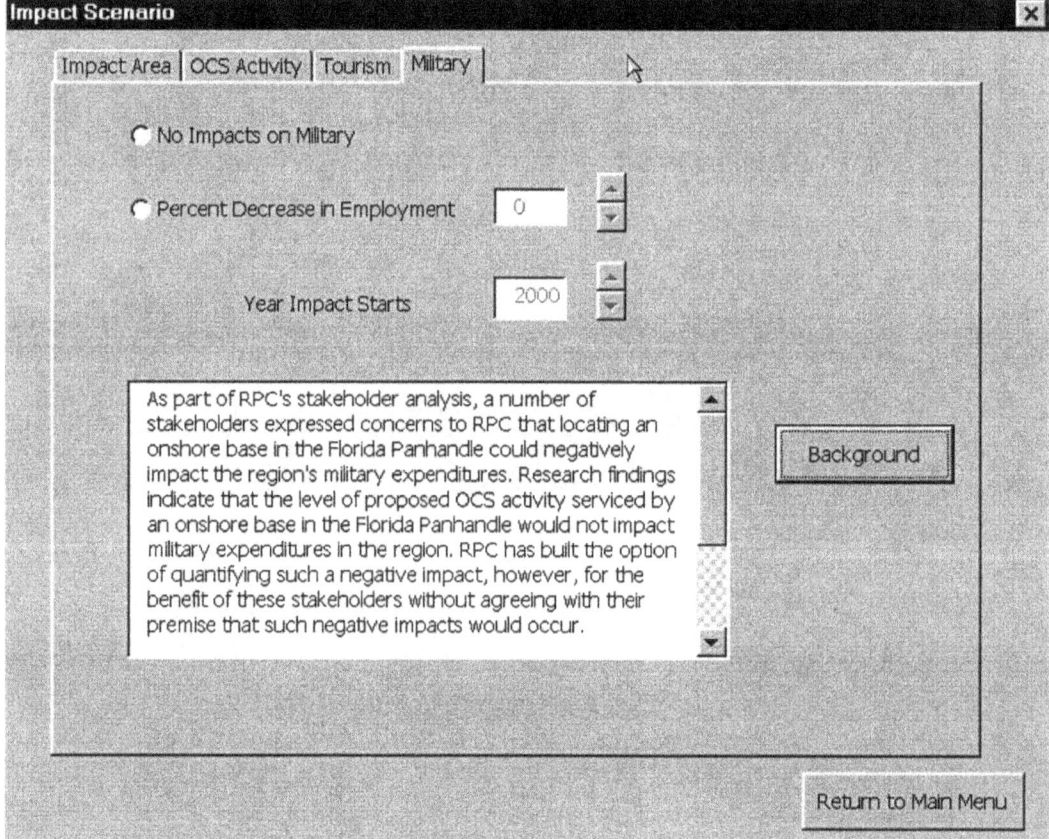

Sample Reports

Users may print reports that detail the impact of the scenario on the metropolitan area chosen. Examples of the reports are printed at the end of the User's Guide (Tables 2-11). Descriptions of each of the reports are as follows:

1. OCS Scenario: This report presents relevant information on the OCS production that would impact the Florida Panhandle. Data include the annual number of boat and helicopter trips to the onshore service base in the Florida Panhandle, the amount of oil and gas production in physical units, and the OCS expenditures in the impact area.

2. Baseline Summary: This report presents output and employment (total and by key industry) for the impact area and population and average annual migration for the impact area and for individual counties.

3. Population: This report compares the population in the baseline and the chosen scenario to estimate the net impact on the study area. The report also estimates the change in households by taking the net impact of the population and dividing by 2.5, which is the average number of people per household in the Florida Panhandle. The report presents the data for the entire area and by county.

4. Employment and Output: This report compares the level of employment and output (1994 millions of dollars) in the baseline and the chosen scenario to estimate the net impact on the study area. The report presents the data for the metropolitan area, not by county.

5. Fiscal Balance: This report presents the impacts of chosen scenarios on the revenues and expenditures of municipal and county governments. The figures on municipal governments are aggregates of all municipal governments within a county. The report presents the data by county in the impact area.

    Expenditures: The model estimates county and municipal expenditures by multiplying the change in population in the chosen scenario by a *per capita* expenditure for county and municipal government for each county.

    Revenues: The model estimates three types of county and municipal revenues:

    (1) residential and commercial & industrial *ad valorem* taxes,

    (2) *per capita* revenues (fees, taxes, licences) multiplied by the change in population, and

15

(3) revenues generated from other sources that government entities would need to offset increased expenditures not offset by the increase in *ad valorem* or *per capita* revenues.

6. Schools: The report presents the data by county (school district) in the impact area.

School-Age Children: The change in school-age children.

Expenditures: The model estimates school district expenditures by multiplying the change in school-age population in the chosen scenario by a *per capita* expenditure per student for each school district.

Revenues: The model estimates three types of school district revenues:

(1) residential and commercial & industrial *ad valorem* taxes,

(2) revenue from the state government per student, and

(3) revenue from the federal government per student.

7. Public Services: This report estimates the change in the following services that would occur in the scenario: amount of residential water consumed, the amount of residential wastewater generated, the amount of solid waste generated, the miles of road and highway constructed, employment in the police department, number of crimes, employment in the fire department, the number of public welfare workers, and the number of physicians. The report presents the data by county in the impact area.

For a more detailed discussion on the assumptions and information used to generate these reports, please read the Final Report associated with the MMS Florida Panhandle model.

Table 2

MMS Florida Panhandle Model - OCS Scenario Report.

Impact Area	Pensacola		Scenario Name:		Scenario One
Report Area	Pensacola		Date:		April 25, 1999
Production Scenario in Lease Sale 181:	Reasonable Maximum		Destin Dome:		Not Serviced in Florida

Item	1995	2000	2005	2010	2015	2020	2025	2030	2035	2040	2045
Oil and Gas Production in Eastern Gulf of Mexico											
Lease Sale 181											
Oil Production (Millions of Barrels)	0.0	0.0	0.0	0.6	1.8	3.3	2.7	2.4	1.5	0.0	0.0
Gas Production (Billions of Cubic Feet)	0.0	0.0	0.0	8.1	28.4	40.5	36.5	32.4	24.3	0.0	0.0
Destin Dome											
Oil Production (Millions of Barrels)	0.0	0.0	0.0	0.0	0.0	0.0	0.0	0.0	0.0	0.0	0.0
Gas Production (Billions Cubic Feet)	0.0	0.0	0.0	0.0	0.0	0.0	0.0	0.0	0.0	0.0	0.0
OCS Expenditures in Impact Area											
Lease Sale 181	0.0	0.0	0.0	2.2	7.3	11.2	9.8	8.7	6.2	0.0	0.0
Destin Dome	0.0	0.0	0.0	0.0	0.0	0.0	0.0	0.0	0.0	0.0	0.0
Scenario Impact on Key Industries											
Tourism											
Percentage Change in Level	0.00%	0.00%	0.00%	0.00%	0.00%	0.00%	0.00%	0.00%	0.00%	0.00%	0.00%
Percentage Change in Growth Rate	0.00%	0.00%	0.00%	0.00%	0.00%	0.00%	0.00%	0.00%	0.00%	0.00%	0.00%
Military											
Percentage Change in Level	0.00%	0.00%	0.00%	0.00%	0.00%	0.00%	0.00%	0.00%	0.00%	0.00%	0.00%
OCS-Related Activities											
Boat Trips from Service Base	0	0	0	288	288	288	288	288	288	0	0
Helicopter Trips from Service Base	0	0	0	1248	1248	1248	1248	1248	1248	0	0

Table 3

MMS Florida Panhandle Model - Baseline Report.

Impact Area Report Areas: Pensacola — Pensacola, Escambia, Santa Rosa

Scenario Name: Scenario One
Date: April 25, 1999

Output ($ Millions)	1995	2000	2005	2010	2015	2020	2025	2030	2035	2040	2045
All	14,451.2	16,449.0	17,223.7	17,974.8	18,766.0	18,951.6	19,143.4	19,599.6	20,067.6	20,547.4	21,039.3
Tourism	248.1	292.4	318.3	340.7	363.5	372.1	381.0	392.5	404.3	416.4	428.9
Military	385.1	422.5	418.6	418.3	425.3	425.3	425.2	426.2	427.2	428.1	429.0
Commercial Fishing	2.9	3.5	3.7	3.9	4.1	4.2	4.3	4.4	4.5	4.6	4.7
Water Transportation	107.0	106.3	109.4	113.4	116.7	116.7	116.7	118.7	120.7	122.7	124.8
Employment	1995	2000	2005	2010	2015	2020	2025	2030	2035	2040	2045
All	193,173	223,342	234,998	245,820	257,169	260,036	262,943	269,060	275,322	281,728	288,279
Tourism	5,265	6,206	6,756	7,231	7,714	7,899	8,086	8,330	8,581	8,838	9,103
Military	10,010	10,966	10,846	10,822	10,987	10,969	10,950	10,959	10,967	10,975	10,981
Fishing	135	159	171	179	187	191	195	200	204	209	214
Water Transportation	509	505	519	537	552	551	550	559	567	576	585
Population	1995	2000	2005	2010	2015	2020	2025	2030	2035	2040	2045
Pensacola	377,822	410,086	441,204	469,488	502,482	526,239	547,200	567,029	584,973	601,966	618,202
Escambia County	281,162	296,578	316,849	334,339	352,894	366,819	379,386	390,820	400,920	410,113	418,437
Santa Rosa County	96,660	113,508	124,354	135,149	149,589	159,420	167,814	176,209	184,053	191,853	199,765
Annual Average Migration	1995	2000	2005	2010	2015	2020	2025	2030	2035	2040	2045
Pensacola	NA	NA	2,760	2,461	3,311	2,033	1,761	2,077	2,200	2,454	2,636
Escambia County	NA	NA	1,518	1,108	1,324	813	704	831	880	982	1,054
Santa Rosa County	NA	NA	1,242	1,354	1,987	1,220	1,056	1,246	1,320	1,472	1,581

18

Table 4

MMS Florida Panhandle Model - Population Report.

Impact Area	Pensacola, Escambia, Santa Rosa		Scenario Name:	Scenario One
Report Areas	Pensacola, Escambia, Santa Rosa		Date:	April 25, 1999

Pensacola Area

	1995	2000	2005	2010	2015	2020	2025	2030	2035	2040	2045
Total Population											
Scenario	377,822	410,086	441,204	469,617	502,964	527,064	548,062	567,882	585,695	602,271	618,377
Baseline	377,822	410,086	441,204	469,488	502,482	526,239	547,200	567,029	584,973	601,966	618,202
Net Change in Population	0	0	0	129	481	825	862	852	722	305	175
Net Change in Households	0	0	0	52	193	330	345	341	289	122	70

Escambia

	1995	2000	2005	2010	2015	2020	2025	2030	2035	2040	2045
Total Population											
Scenario	281,162	296,578	316,849	334,395	353,088	367,152	379,746	391,194	401,254	410,288	418,557
Baseline	281,162	296,578	316,849	334,339	352,894	366,819	379,386	390,820	400,920	410,113	418,437
Net Change in Population	0	0	0	57	195	333	360	374	334	174	121
Net Change in Households	0	0	0	23	78	133	144	150	134	70	48

Santa Rosa

	1995	2000	2005	2010	2015	2020	2025	2030	2035	2040	2045
Total Population											
Scenario	96,660	113,508	124,354	135,222	149,875	159,912	168,316	176,688	184,441	191,983	199,820
Baseline	96,660	113,508	124,354	135,149	149,589	159,420	167,814	176,209	184,053	191,853	199,765
Net Change in Population	0	0	0	73	287	492	502	479	388	131	55
Net Change in Households	0	0	0	29	115	197	201	191	155	52	22

Table 5

MMS Florida Panhandle Model - Output and Employment Report.

Impact Area	Pensacola										
Report Area	Pensacola										

Scenario Name: Scenario One
Date: April 25, 1999

	1995	2000	2005	2010	2015	2020	2025	2030	2035	2040	2045
Total Output (in $ Millions)											
Scenario	14,451.2	16,449.0	17,223.7	17,978.0	18,777.3	18,969.1	19,158.7	19,613.1	20,077.1	20,547.4	21,039.3
Baseline	14,451.2	16,449.0	17,223.7	17,974.8	18,766.0	18,951.6	19,143.4	19,599.6	20,067.6	20,547.4	21,039.3
Net Impact	0.0	0.0	0.0	3.2	11.3	17.5	15.3	13.6	9.6	0.0	0.0
Output Excl. Gov.											
Scenario	12,703.5	14,354.2	15,093.7	15,816.6	16,562.8	16,760.1	16,955.8	17,379.1	17,811.6	18,250.2	18,709.8
Baseline	12,703.5	14,354.2	15,093.7	15,813.5	16,551.6	16,742.8	16,940.7	17,365.7	17,802.1	18,250.2	18,709.8
Net Impact	0.0	0.0	0.0	3.1	11.2	17.3	15.1	13.4	9.5	0.0	0.0
Employment											
Scenario	193,173	223,342	234,998	245,930	257,548	260,621	263,454	269,514	275,644	281,728	288,279
Baseline	193,173	223,342	234,998	245,820	257,169	260,036	262,943	269,060	275,322	281,728	288,279
Net Impact	0	0	0	110	380	584	511	454	322	0	0

Table 6

MMS Florida Panhandle Model - Fiscal Balance Report (Escambia County).

Impact Area Report Area	Pensacola Escambia County					Scenario Name: Date:		Scenario One April 25, 1999			
Item	1995	2000	2005	2010	2015	2020	2025	2030	2035	2040	2045
Scenario Population	281,162	296,57	316,84	334,395	353,088	367,152	379,746	391,194	401,254	410,288	418,55
Baseline Population	281,162	296,57	316,84	334,339	352,894	366,819	379,386	390,820	400,920	410,113	418,43
Net Change in Population	0	0	0	57	195	333	360	374	334	174	121
Net Change in Households	0	0	0	23	78	133	144	150	134	70	48
Net Change in Area Output Excluding Govt (in Millions of Dollars)	0	0	0	3	11	17	15	13	9	0	0
County Government											
Revenues	0	0	0	40,484	138,905	237,812	257,273	266,923	238,500	124,487	86,165
Ad Valorem Taxes	0	0	0	9,183	31,844	53,154	54,825	55,205	47,478	21,130	14,625
Residential	0	0	0	6,871	23,577	40,365	43,668	45,306	40,481	21,130	14,625
Commercial and Industrial	0	0	0	2,311	8,267	12,789	11,158	9,899	6,997	0	0
Other Taxes, Fees, Licences, etc.	0	0	0	17,370	59,598	102,033	110,383	114,524	102,329	53,411	36,969
From All Other Sources to Balance Budget	0	0	0	13,931	47,464	82,624	92,064	97,195	88,693	49,946	34,571
Expenditures	0	0	0	40,484	138,905	237,812	257,273	266,923	238,500	124,487	86,165
Municipal Government											
Revenues	0	0	0	33,021	113,301	193,976	209,850	217,721	194,538	101,541	70,282
Ad Valorem Taxes	0	0	0	1,196	4,147	6,922	7,140	7,189	6,183	2,752	1,905
Residential	0	0	0	895	3,070	5,257	5,687	5,900	5,272	2,752	1,905
Commercial and Industrial	0	0	0	301	1,077	1,666	1,453	1,289	911	0	0
Other Taxes, Fees, Licences, etc.	0	0	0	14,879	51,051	87,401	94,533	98,100	87,654	45,752	31,668
From All Other Sources to Balance Budget	0	0	0	16,947	58,103	99,653	108,157	112,432	100,701	53,036	36,710
Expenditures	0	0	0	33,021	113,301	193,976	209,850	217,721	194,538	101,541	70,28

Table 7

MMS Florida Panhandle Model - Fiscal Balance Report (Santa Rosa County).

Impact Area / Report Area: Pensacola, Santa Rosa County

Scenario Name: Scenario One
Date: April 25, 1999

Item	1995	2000	2005	2010	2015	2020	2025	2030	2035	2040	2045
Scenario Population	96,660	113,508	124,35	135,222	149,875	159,912	168,316	176,688	184,441	191,983	199,820
Baseline Population	96,660	113,508	124,35	135,149	149,589	159,420	167,814	176,209	184,053	191,853	199,765
Net Change in Population	0	0	0	73	287	492	502	479	388	131	55
Net Change in Households	0	0	0	29	115	197	201	191	155	52	22
Net Change in Area Output Excluding Govt (in Millions of $)											
County Government											
Revenues	0	0	0	54,374	214,533	367,914	375,045	357,817	289,971	97,608	40,901
Ad Valorem Taxes	0	0	0	8,100	31,804	54,289	55,000	52,338	42,227	13,786	5,777
Residential	0	0	0	7,680	30,300	51,964	52,971	50,538	40,955	13,786	5,777
Commercial and Industrial	0	0	0	420	1,503	2,326	2,029	1,800	1,272	0	0
Other Taxes, Fees, Licences	0	0	0	25,642	101,169	173,500	176,863	168,739	136,744	46,030	19,288
From All Other Sources to Balance Budget	0	0	0	20,632	81,560	140,124	143,182	136,741	110,999	37,972	15,836
Expenditures	0	0	0	54,374	214,533	367,914	375,045	357,817	289,971	97,608	40,901
Municipal Government											
Revenues	0	0	0	18,182	71,737	123,026	125,411	119,650	96,963	32,639	13,677
Ad Valorem Taxes	0	0	0	343	1,345	2,296	2,326	2,213	1,786	583	244
Residential	0	0	0	325	1,281	2,197	2,240	2,137	1,732	583	244
Commercial and Industrial	0	0	0	18	64	98	86	76	54	0	0
Other Taxes, Fees, Licences,	0	0	0	10,360	40,876	70,100	71,459	68,176	55,249	18,598	7,793
From All Other Sources to Balance Budget	0	0	0	7,479	29,517	50,630	51,626	49,260	39,928	13,458	5,639
Expenditure	0	0	0	18,182	71,737	123,026	125,411	119,650	96,963	32,639	13,677

Table 8

MMS Florida Panhandle Model - Schools Report (Escambia County).

| Impact Area | Pensacola | | | | | | Scenario Name: | Scenario One | | | |
| Report Area | Escambia County | | | | | | Date: | April 25, 1999 | | | |
	1995	2000	2005	2010	2015	2020	2025	2030	2035	2040	2045
Number of School-Age Children											
Scenario	55,401	59,473	57,103	59,513	64,247	67,319	68,574	68,661	68,579	69,718	71,906
Baseline	55,401	59,473	57,103	59,494	64,200	67,264	68,534	68,593	68,496	69,672	71,857
Net Change	0	0	0	18	47	56	40	68	83	47	48
Net Change in Households	0	0	0	23	78	133	144	150	134	70	48
Fiscal Impact of Net Change											
Revenues	0	0	0	80,652	213,095	266,657	207,706	322,182	375,211	208,771	208,369
Local Ad Valorem Taxes	0	0	0	10,634	36,875	61,552	63,487	63,926	54,979	24,468	16,936
Residential Property	0	0	0	7,957	27,302	46,742	50,567	52,464	46,877	24,468	16,936
Commercial Property	0	0	0	2,677	9,573	14,810	12,920	11,463	8,102	0	0
State Revenues	0	0	0	62,429	159,556	188,859	134,948	231,629	281,967	158,276	164,399
Federal Revenues	0	0	0	10,266	26,237	31,056	22,191	38,089	46,367	26,027	27,034
Expenditures	0	0	0	88,050	225,038	266,368	190,332	326,692	397,688	223,233	231,870

Table 9

MMS Florida Panhandle Model - Schools Report (Santa Rosa County).

Impact Area	Pensacola								Scenario Name:	Scenario One	
Report Area	Santa Rosa County								Date:	April 25, 1999	
	1995	2000	2005	2010	2015	2020	2025	2030	2035	2040	2045
Number of School-Age Children											
Scenario	19,462	21,262	22,059	23,045	24,690	26,073	27,190	28,215	29,040	29,938	31,249
Baseline	19,462	21,262	22,059	23,036	24,656	26,008	27,108	28,125	28,969	29,913	31,249
Net Change	0	0	0	8	34	65	82	90	71	25	0
Net Change in Households	0	0	0	29	115	197	201	191	155	52	22
Fiscal Impact of Net Change											
Revenues	0	0	0	29,153	117,737	217,758	258,156	273,514	218,545	75,328	7,312
Local Ad Valorem Taxes	0	0	0	10,277	40,352	68,882	69,783	66,405	53,578	17,492	7,329
Residential Property	0	0	0	9,744	38,445	65,931	67,209	64,122	51,963	17,492	7,329
Commercial Property	0	0	0	533	1,907	2,951	2,574	2,284	1,614	0	0
State Revenues	0	0	0	15,364	62,768	120,186	151,154	165,755	131,866	45,783	(14)
Federal Revenues	0	0	0	4,045	16,525	31,641	39,793	43,638	34,716	12,053	(4)
Expenditures	0	0	0	36,506	149,137	285,565	359,144	393,837	313,316	108,782	(34)

Table 10

MMS Florida Panhandle Model - Public Services Report (Escambia County).

Impact Area Report Area	Pensacola Escambia County								Scenario Name: Date:	Scenario One April 25, 1999	
	1995	2000	2005	2010	2015	2020	2025	2030	2035	2040	2045
Population											
Scenario	281,162	296,578	316,849	334,395	353,088	367,152	379,746	391,194	401,254	410,288	418,557
Baseline	281,162	296,578	316,849	334,339	352,894	366,819	379,386	390,820	400,920	410,113	418,437
Net Impact	0	0	0	57	195	333	360	374	334	174	121
Public Services Impact											
Residential Water (thousands of gallons per day)	0.0	0.0	0.0	4.7	16.3	27.9	30.1	31.3	27.9	14.6	10.1
Residential Wastewater (thousands of gallons per day)	0.0	0.0	0.0	4.0	13.9	23.8	25.7	26.7	23.8	12.4	8.6
Solid Waste (tons per year)	0.0	0.0	0.0	90.7	311.2	532.8	576.4	598.0	534.4	278.9	193.1
Road & Highway (miles)	0.0	0.0	0.0	0.2	0.7	1.2	1.3	1.4	1.2	0.7	0.5
Police Protection	0	0	0	0	0	1	1	1	1	0	0
Crimes	0.0	0.0	0.0	3.5	12.1	20.6	22.3	23.2	20.7	10.8	7.5
Fire Protection	0	0	0	0	0	0	0	0	0	0	0
Public Welfare	0	0	0	0	0	0	0	0	0	0	0
Physicians	0	0	0	0	0	1	1	1	1	0	0

Table 11

MMS Florida Panhandle Model – Public Services Report (Santa Rosa County).

| Impact Area | Pensacola | | | | | | | | Scenario Name: | Scenario One | |
| Report Area | Santa Rosa County | | | | | | | | Date: | April 25, 1999 | |

Population	1995	2000	2005	2010	2015	2020	2025	2030	2035	2040	2045
Scenario	96,660	113,508	124,354	135,222	149,875	159,912	168,316	176,688	184,441	191,983	199,820
Baseline	96,660	113,508	124,354	135,149	149,589	159,420	167,814	176,209	184,053	191,853	199,765
Net Impact	0	0	0	73	287	492	502	479	388	131	55

Public Services Impact

	1995	2000	2005	2010	2015	2020	2025	2030	2035	2040	2045
Residential Water (thousands gallons per day)	0.0	0.0	0.0	6.7	26.2	45.0	45.9	43.8	35.5	11.9	5.0
Residential Wastewater (thousands of gallons per day)	0.0	0.0	0.0	2.2	8.6	14.8	15.1	14.4	11.7	3.9	1.6
Solid Waste (tons per year)	0	0	0	54	212	364	371	354	287	97	40
Road & Highway (miles)	0.0	0.0	0.0	0.5	2.0	3.5	3.6	3.4	2.7	0.9	0.4
Police Protection	0	0	0	0	1	1	1	1	1	0	0
Crimes	0	0	0	3	10	18	18	17	14	5	2
Fire Protection	0	0	0	0	0	0	0	0	0	0	0
Public Welfare	0	0	0	0	0	0	0	0	0	0	0
Physicians	0	0	0	0	0	1	1	1	0	0	0

The Department of the Interior Mission

As the Nation's principal conservation agency, the Department of the Interior has responsibility for most of our nationally owned public lands and natural resources. This includes fostering sound use of our land and water resources; protecting our fish, wildlife, and biological diversity; preserving the environmental and cultural values of our national parks and historical places; and providing for the enjoyment of life through outdoor recreation. The Department assesses our energy and mineral resources and works to ensure that their development is in the best interests of all our people by encouraging stewardship and citizen participation in their care. The Department also has a major responsibility for American Indian reservation communities and for people who live in island territories under U.S. administration.

The Minerals Management Service Mission

As a bureau of the Department of the Interior, the Minerals Management Service's (MMS) primary responsibilities are to manage the mineral resources located on the Nation's Outer Continental Shelf (OCS), collect revenue from the Federal OCS and onshore Federal and Indian lands, and distribute those revenues.

Moreover, in working to meet its responsibilities, the **Offshore Minerals Management Program** administers the OCS competitive leasing program and oversees the safe and environmentally sound exploration and production of our Nation's offshore natural gas, oil and other mineral resources. The MMS **Minerals Revenue Management** meets its responsibilities by ensuring the efficient, timely and accurate collection and disbursement of revenue from mineral leasing and production due to Indian tribes and allottees, States and the U.S. Treasury.

The MMS strives to fulfill its responsibilities through the general guiding principles of: (1) being responsive to the public's concerns and interests by maintaining a dialogue with all potentially affected parties and (2) carrying out its programs with an emphasis on working to enhance the quality of life for all Americans by lending MMS assistance and expertise to economic development and environmental protection.